Dedication

Psalms 46:5
"God is within her; she will not fail."

Ephesians 3:20
"Now to Him who is able to do immeasurably more than all we
can ask or imagine…"

To my dad that now lives in heaven. I am so blessed to have had
you as a father and a friend. You embodied the true essence of
kindness.

To my mom thank you for always believing in me and being the
driving force of what a Proverbs' 31 Woman is.

To my husband, thank you for always reminding me the
importance of James 2:26.

To my three heart beats Dillon, Justin, and Presten. Thank you
for being my inspiration for my first children's book. I promise
to continue to keep writing and keep making you proud.

Ordering Information:
For details, contact- ms.rosiesbooks@gmail.com
Print ISBN: 979-8-3304-8080-7
Ebook ISBN: 979-8-3304-8081-4

Ms. Rosie
and the
Kingdom of Kindness

Written By

Rose Jules Antenor

Illustrated by Travis A. Thompson

Welcome friends to the Kingdom of Kindness!

Where caring deeply for people near and far shows that you're a kindness superstar.

So, come inside and you will find that in the kingdom,

kindness will always be your guide.

In your heart you will discover...

To use kind words.
Mean words are not okay,
no matter what occurred.

You're Dumb!
That's not nice.
Use kind words.

To apologize when you're wrong. Saying "I'm sorry" only makes you strong.

To practice patience,
it may be difficult when
you try at first.
Over time your patience will
grow and burst.

I know I can do this.
I did it!

To say "please" and "thank you". Displaying manners makes you exceptionally great!

To be respectful towards others, whether they're big or small, everyone deserves to be respected after all.

To show compassion and empathy when others are feeling sad and lonely.

To be grateful for
all your blessings.
Whether big or small
you should appreciate them all!

To speak up when
something is wrong.
Your voice is important.
So, speak with courage and let
your words be strong.

Now take your guide and
place it close to your heart.
Keep it close and
never let it depart.
Then soon you will see
that you're a kindness superstar
just like me!

Welcome to the Kingdom of Kindness

Remember You're a Kindness Superstar

Always Remeber to:

- Use Kind Words
- Apologize
- Be Patient
- Say Please and Thank you
- Be Respectful
- Be Compassionate
- Be Grateful
- Speak Up

Rose J. Antenor has had a passion for children's literature since she started her teaching career twenty-one years ago. Rose loves inspiring young children. She hopes that this book encourages children to practice kindness and be the difference that the world needs. With beautiful illustrations and heartfelt characters, Rose aims to inspire readers to be kind. She treasures time with her family and energetic growing boys.